FARMING AND THE ENVIRONMENT

Mark Lambert

Acid Rain
Conserving the Atmosphere
Conserving the Polar Regions
Conserving Rainforests
Protecting the Oceans
Protecting Wildlife
The Spread of Deserts
Waste and Recycling

Cover: Pineapple fields encroach on rainforest in
Queensland, Australia

Series editor: Sue Hadden
Series designer: Ross George

First published in 1990 by
Wayland (Publishers) Ltd
61 Western Road, Hove
East Sussex BN3 1JD, England

© Copyright 1990 Wayland (Publishers) Ltd

This edition published in 1991 by
Wayland (Publishers) Ltd

British Library Cataloguing in Publication Data
Lambert, Mark, 1946-
    Farming and the environment. –
    1. Agricultural industries, Environmental aspects.
    I. Title   II. Series
    338.1

HARDBACK ISBN 1-85210-828-2

PAPERBACK ISBN 0-7502-0279-3

Typeset by Rachel Gibbs, Wayland.
Printed in Italy by G. Canale C.S.p.A., Turin

Contents

Farming is a way of life that has been practised for over 9,000 years. And from the moment that people first settled down and began cultivating the land, they started to alter their surroundings. For thousands of years forests have been cut down to make way for fields. In this and many other ways farming has always had a marked effect upon the environment.

The origins of farming

Early humans were wandering hunters. They followed the animals they hunted, such as deer, bison and other wild cattle, as they migrated from place to place in search of fresh grass. Then, about 12,000 years ago, people discovered that they could tame animals such as goats and sheep sufficiently to keep them in flocks or herds.

Life now became a little easier, but people still lived a nomadic existence. They continued to move from place to place, taking their flocks of domesticated animals with them and gathering wild plants to add to their diet. Then, about 9,000 years ago in the Middle East, a rapid change occurred — one that would literally alter the face of the earth.

All over the world farming has changed the landscape. In Montana, USA, land that was natural grassland is now used to grow wheat.

Above *Bread wheat (**left**) has plumper grains than emmer (**right**).*

Above *Today's bread wheat developed from the accidental interbreeding of wild forms of wheat. Farmers prize it for its full head of plump grains.*

One of the wild plants that had become important to these people was wheat. This was a type of wild grass, but its fruits (grains) could be ground up to make bread, a very useful food. Wheat became so important that people began to make harvesting tools, such as sickles constructed from bone and pieces of flint. However, no one thought of sowing some of the seed in order to grow new plants. The plants scattered their own seed so well that there seemed little point in doing it for them.

At this point, however, nature took a hand, bringing about not one but two remarkable changes. First, wild wheat accidentally interbred with another kind of grass. This probably happened frequently, but in most cases the result would have been a hybrid plant that could not reproduce itself. In this case, however, the new plant could produce seeds. And the grains were much plumper than those of ordinary wild wheat and were, therefore, even more worthwhile gathering.

This was not the end of the story. The new plant, known as emmer, then interbred with another kind of grass, producing a new hybrid plant with even plumper grains. This was bread wheat and, by a freak of nature, it too was able to reproduce itself. But unlike wild wheat and Emmer, bread wheat could not easily spread its own seeds. So, in order to obtain a good supply of bread wheat, people had to sow the seed themselves. Bread wheat was clearly a plant worth cultivating, and so farming began.

Cultivating the land

Farming developed in many different parts of the world. Different peoples learned how to grow a variety of native crops, such as peas, beans, peppers and gourds. But the most important crops were the cereals. In Europe and Asia farmers grew wheat, barley, rice and millet. On the other side of the world, the cultivation of maize spread from Mexico into both North and South America.

In Europe and Asia farming spread gradually.

Peruvian Indians drying out a new crop of maize in the Andes.

Farming settlements appeared in south-eastern Europe about 8,000 years ago, but farming did not reach northern Europe for another 3,000 years. With farming came the village way of life. People lived in permanent settlements, cultivating the land around them for about ten years until the soil became exhausted. Then they moved on to another area, leaving the soil to recover — a process that could take many years.

One of the few remaining ancient beech woods in Europe. Most of the beech woods that exist today were planted by people.

At this stage most of Europe was covered by broadleaved forest. This has been the natural vegetation of this part of the world since the land warmed up after the end of the last ice age some 10,000 years ago. Left to itself, today's European countryside would eventually become covered in trees again. The process of deforestation was begun by the early settlers. Natural clearings in the forest were grazed by deer. Early farmers probably took advantage of such clearings, expanding them to create more room for growing crops and grazing domesticated animals. Trees were felled with stone axes or stripped of their bark and allowed to die. Scrub was often removed by burning. By bringing in herds of domestic animals to graze, the cleared areas were enlarged. This process has been going on for thousands of years, and as the population of Europe increased, more and more land was cleared. Today in Europe, little of the original ancient forest remains. Most of the woodland that exists today has been planted by people.

Sheep grazing on English downland. Very few trees remain on these chalk grassland areas.

The countryside today

The removal of trees has not been without some benefits. The farming systems developed over the years have introduced a great deal of variety into our countryside. A number of the wildlife habitats that we now regard as important are the direct result of farming practices. Hedgerows provide an excellent refuge for the animals and plants that formerly inhabited the edges of forests and clearings. Much of the land that is now heathland and moorland was once farmed. As elsewhere, the trees were felled, but on sandy or rocky ground the soil was poor and soon became unsuitable for growing crops. When it was abandoned by the farmers, only low-growing, scrubby plants, such as heather and gorse, could survive on the exhausted soil. Today, heathland contains a variety of unique animals and plants.

The grasslands created by early farmers have also developed their own unique features. Traditional meadows cut for hay in late June or July allow a wide range of plants to flower and produce seed for the next season.

When sheep are put out to graze on chalk grassland, they benefit the chalk-loving wild flowers. The grazing keeps the grass sufficiently short to allow the wild flowers to survive and bloom in profusion.

A threatened world

Unfortunately, habitats both old and new are under threat throughout the world. The world's population is increasing — by the year 2000 it is expected to rise by 1,000 million to about 6,000 million. Therefore, more and more food will be needed. Today's intensive farming, based on the use of machines and chemicals, is designed to produce more out of the land than ever before. As a result, there is less room left for wildlife. Meadows brimming with colourful summer flowers were a common sight before the Second World War. Since then, however, the introduction

Typical heathland plants, such as gorse and heather, survive on poor soils. Heathland like this is also home to a variety of unique animals.

of chemical weedkillers has meant that most natural grassland meadows have disappeared. The world's remaining forests are being destroyed at an increasing rate, grazing land is being turned into desert, and today's farming methods are adding to the world's pollution problems. The need to supply the world with food is now not just changing the landscape; it is destroying the environment.

Hedges

Hedges were originally planted by farmers as natural fences. A well maintained hedge stops domestic animals from straying on to another farmer's land. It also provides a refuge for wildlife. Hedges may contain several kinds of shrub and tree, while smaller flowering plants, ferns and mosses can grow in the shelter at the bottom of the hedge. The hedge also serves as a home for birds and small mammals, and a host of insects feed on the plants. A hedge acts as a barrier to the wind. It thus provides shelter for domestic stock and, where the land is ploughed up for cultivation, it helps to prevent the soil being blown away.

Removing a hedgerow, therefore, has a considerable effect upon the local environment. The wildlife disappears and any exposed soil is more easily eroded by the wind.

The hedges that remain today are usually trimmed using a flail cutter, operated by a farm tractor. This method produces neat hedges, but does little for the wildlife. Hedges are often trimmed too low to form an effective barrier to the wind. Heavily trimmed hedges offer little protection to birds and other animals. Constant trimming helps to weaken a hedge and eventually it cannot hold the animals in the field.

Right *The woodmouse is one of many animals that have adapted to life in hedgerows.*

Below left *In spring British hedgerow plants include foxgloves and honeysuckle.*

Below right *A tractor using a flail hedgetrimmer. Hedges heavily cut in this way offer little protection for wildlife.*

Farming and pollution

Pollution is now a serious problem in many parts of the world. Much of it is caused by the industrial processes used to generate energy and produce the materials we use. However, modern farming practices are also polluting the environment.

Many of the materials that we call pollutants already exist in nature. However, such materials can easily become pollutants when present in unnaturally large amounts. The chemicals known as nitrates, for example, occur naturally in the ground, and are actually essential for plant growth. For this reason farmers add large amounts of nitrate-containing fertilizers to the soil, in order to make their crops grow. The plants rapidly take up the chemicals in the fertilizer and develop into stronger plants that produce better yields than those left untreated.

Unfortunately, not all the nitrates are taken up by the plants. The process takes about three days and, in the meantime, rain may wash nitrates out of the topsoil. This is a particular problem in places where the soil is very well drained. In such places, farmers have to apply large quantities of fertilizer to ensure the crop takes up enough. The remaining nitrates from the fertilizer run via ditches and streams into ponds and lakes.

A farmer spreading nitrogen-containing fertilizer in Maryland, USA. In this case the fertilizer is a liquid form of ammonia, which will be converted into nitrates by bacteria in the soil.

Stagnant ponds and lakes

Nitrogen and phosphorus, in the form of the chemicals known as nitrates and phosphates, help plants to grow. However, if these nutrient chemicals accumulate in slow-moving water, algae (simple water plants) use them as a source of food and multiply rapidly. The lake soon becomes choked by a green slimy mass of these algae. This process is called eutrophication.

The algae use up some of the oxygen dissolved in the water, but during the hours of daylight at least they also produce oxygen, as a result of the food-making process called photosynthesis. After a while, however, the algae start to die and fall to the bottom of the lake. There large numbers of bacteria feed on the dead plant material and these bacteria take large amounts of oxygen from the water. They use up so much oxygen that there is none left for other living things, such as fish, water snails and insects, which also die. The bacteria thrive and the pond or lake rapidly becomes stagnant and lifeless.

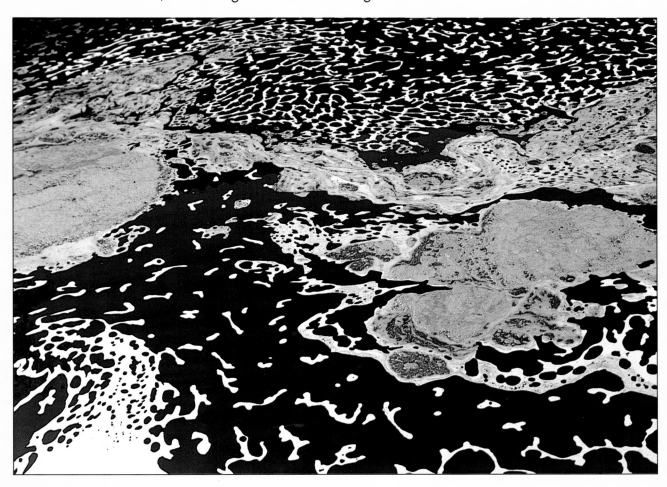

A pond suffering from the effects of eutrophication. The surface is covered by a green algal scum and the water is stagnant and lifeless.

Nitrates are also washed into the groundwater and into rivers, both of which are used as sources of drinking water. High levels of nitrate in drinking water are thought to be causing several problems. When nitrates are taken into the digestive system of a human, bacteria convert them into nitrites. These chemicals prevent the blood from taking up oxygen properly, and can be dangerous in large amounts. The problem is rare in adults, but babies are known to be especially at risk. Nitrites are also suspected of helping to cause cancer.

Artificial fertilizers are not the only source of nitrates. They are also present in naturally-produced farmyard manures, which have been used by farmers for hundreds of years. Where animals spend the winter in sheds, bedded down on straw, their dung becomes mixed with the straw and forms manure. Used in moderation,

A slurry pit is used to collect the water and dung that drains from a cattle yard. Leakage of slurry can pollute ditches and rivers.

farmyard manures produce little in the way of pollution. They release their plant nutrients more slowly than artificial fertilizers, and the organic (plant-derived) material in manures helps to improve the soil. However, if they are used excessively, manures can add to the problem of nitrate pollution.

Today, however, farmyard manures are used less often. Modern farming practices generate much more concentrated materials known as slurries — semi-liquid materials composed almost entirely of dung and urine. Slurries are produced by animals that are farmed intensively (in large numbers), such as cattle and pigs. These animals are kept in great numbers inside special housing, where they are fed on concentrated feeds. Of course, the animals produce huge quantities of waste materials. In some places, disposing of large amounts of slurry has become a major problem. In the Netherlands in 1986, pig farmers produced 97 million tonnes of slurry, 28 million tonnes more than they could deal with by themselves.

Animal slurry is rapidly becoming a serious threat to the environment. Like human sewage, it is a mass of decomposing material. The bacteria that carry out the process of decomposition need large amounts of oxygen. Human sewage is sent to sewage works for treatment. But slurries, which are produced in far greater quantities than human sewage, are stored on the farms themselves in pits or tanks. All too often, these containers leak or are allowed to overflow, causing severe pollution of neighbouring streams and rivers. Fish and other animals die of suffocation, as their oxygen is removed. Untreated slurry is often sprayed directly on to fields, from where it may then be washed off by rain into rivers. Decomposing animal waste also produces large amounts of methane, which is one of the gases causing the greenhouse effect (see page 43).

Even worse pollution can be caused by the farm liquid known as silage effluent. Silage is a winter feed made by fermenting freshly cut grass. The fermentation process produces a very acid liquid, called the effluent. Made properly, silage produces very little effluent. However, if the grass is too wet, or is not left in the field to wilt properly, large quantities of effluent are produced. Like slurries, silage effluent is sprayed on fields and is sometimes allowed to run into streams and rivers.

Silage is made by heaping up finely-chopped grass. After being rolled by a tractor, the grass is sealed under polythene to keep out the air.

Biocides

The crops that farmers grow are not just a source of food for humans. They also provide a well-stocked, easily available larder for a host of other living things, for example insect pests. Some of these can devastate crops, and farmers therefore wage war upon them. The weapons they use are chemicals that kill living organisms — biocides.

There are three main groups of organisms on which biocides are used. Weeds are simply plants growing where they are not wanted. For example, many grow among newly-sown crops and use up some of the soil nutrients. Their seeds may also become mixed up with grain at harvest time. The chemicals used to deal with such plants are called herbicides.

Many crop plants are also attacked by parasitic fungi. These are plant-like organisms that live by taking nutrients from the bodies of green plants. Such fungi include a number of mildews, moulds and rusts, which can cause severe damage to crops. Farmers, therefore, treat crops with fungicides to prevent attack. However, the most devastating attacks on crop plants are usually carried out by animal pests, most of which are insects. These animals feed on the leaves, roots, sap, fruits and seeds of plants, and may cause a great deal of damage. Farmers wage war on them with pesticides — poisonous chemicals designed to kill animal life.

Farmers use fungicides to prevent crop diseases. Here the fungus known as corn smut has made this head of maize totally unfit for use.

Many farmers and growers regard biocides as being absolutely essential. Unfortunately, their use does have a considerable effect upon the environment. They are generally sprayed over crops, but this method almost inevitably means that some of the spray drifts away from the area intended. A large number of wild plants that live

In northern Africa swarms of locusts often devastate vital crops, leaving farmers little alternative to using pesticides like dieldrin.

in fields and hedges are becoming rare, as so many are killed by herbicides. Some herbicides are also harmful to animals and humans.

Pesticides are even more dangerous. They are very poisonous chemicals, many of which remain in the environment for a long time. Pesticides are washed off the land and eventually end up in rivers and seas, where they poison fish and other water animals. Drifting spray causes many accidental poisonings of humans, including both farm workers and people passing by. Many pesticides contain chemicals that are suspected of being able to cause cancer in humans.

The most notorious pesticides are the organochlorines, such as DDT and dieldrin. Small amounts of these chemicals build up in the

Spraying crops in Gansu, China, without the protection of a mask. Every year thousands of people are poisoned by pesticides.

bodies of animals and are passed on up the food chain to predators, such as badgers and birds of prey. The organochlorines then become concentrated in the bodies of these animals, with the result that they die or become unable to breed. Their use is now banned in many developed countries, but because they are cheap, they are still being used in some places, particularly the poorer parts of the world.

16

Throughout the world over 2 million tonnes of pesticide are used each year, and it is estimated that 20,000 deaths a year occur due to pesticide poisoning. Pesticides and their residues are also present in some human foods. In some parts of the world, organochlorines are known to be accumulating in the bodies of humans.

Some insect pests have become resistant to the insecticides used against them. In such cases farmers either have to use larger amounts or find a new insecticide, in either case adding to the problem of pollution.

This diagram shows how organochlorine pesticides, such as DDT and dieldrin, tend to accumulate in food chains, poisoning many animals in the process.

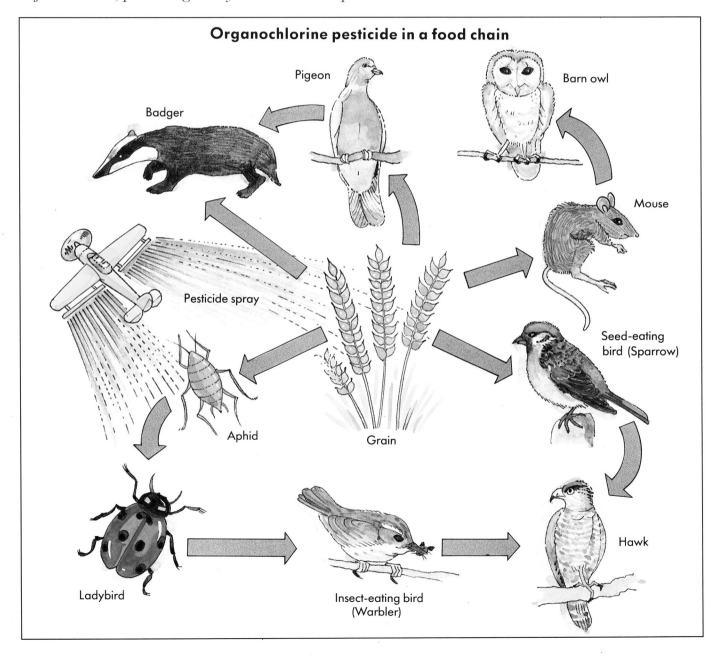

Organochlorine pesticide in a food chain

Pigeon

Barn owl

Badger

Mouse

Pesticide spray

Seed-eating bird (Sparrow)

Aphid

Grain

Ladybird

Insect-eating bird (Warbler)

Hawk

Farming and wildlife

Wild flowers of alpine hay meadows are allowed to set seed before they are cut with the grass.

It is often difficult to meet the needs of both farming and wildlife. Wild animals and plants need suitable habitats in which to live, but these are generally very different to the areas needed for farming. Thus humans have competed with nature for space since farming began. Inevitably, humans have nearly always won this competition, but in the past it has generally been possible for farming and wildlife to exist alongside each other without too much difficulty. In recent years, however, the balance has altered. Changing farm practices and the fact that more and more of the world's land is now being used to grow food, mean that there are now fewer and fewer places where wildlife can exist.

Today hay meadows are a rare sight. They have been replaced with large fields of single crops, such as rape, wheat and grass for silage.

For example, more of the world's grassland, both natural and man-made, is being ploughed up to plant crops. Much of the grassland that remains is now overgrazed, with the result that many wild plants are disappearing. In temperate countries hay has long been the traditional winter feed. Today, more and more animals are fed on silage made from grass. The grass is cut several times during the summer months, and fields cut in this way do not have the wild flowers found in hay meadows. Large amounts of manure and artificial fertilizer are spread on the land to produce more grass. This results in the disappearance of wild plants that cannot tolerate high levels of nitrogen, and cannot compete with the vigorous growth of grass.

A forage harvester collecting grass for silage. Cutting grass two or three times a year to make silage allows few wild flowers to survive.

Disappearing wildlife

Throughout the world there are animals and plants in danger of extinction; many are already extinct. One of the reasons for the disappearance of many animals is that they have been overexploited — hunted for food or to provide prized articles such as furs, skins, shells, tusks and horns. Others have disappeared because they have either been preyed on or could not compete with animals introduced by humans.

But the main reason for the disappearance of animals and plants is simply that their habitats have been destroyed. And in many cases the reason for this destruction has been to clear more land for farming. This is not, of course, a new occurrence; habitat destruction has been going on for thousands of years. The problem is, however, that we are still destroying wildlife habitats at an alarming rate.

The disappearing barn owl

The barn owl was once one of the world's commonest owls, but like many birds of prey, its numbers have declined because of today's farming practices. It has become much rarer in Europe. However, it is an unusual case, because farming seems to have been the cause of it becoming common in the first place.

In completely natural landscapes, barn owls nest in cliffs and hollow trees. They hunt in open spaces for voles, mice and other small mammals. When humans began to create fields, the hunting grounds of barn owls became larger. And the barns built by farmers to shelter their animals and store food provided excellent nesting sites. Grain spilt on the barn floors attracted mice and rats, which provided more food for the owls. Over the years the barn owl actually became dependent on human farming activities.

More recently, however, farming has become more efficient. The old, cosy barns have been demolished and replaced by draughty, open barns. Hollow trees are generally removed, less grain is spilled, and today's fields are less attractive to small mammals. This beautiful bird has thus become a victim of its own dependence on

humans. The use of pesticides has also contributed to its decline (see page 16), because the bird absorbs dangerous amounts of these through the food chain. One effect of pesticides on owls is that they lay eggs with very thin shells, and the young owls inside them are sometimes deformed.

Barn owls have now become rare in much of Europe. Recently the Royal Society for the Protection of Birds has launched a scheme encouraging farmers to take steps to help these superb owls that were once so common in the countryside.

What happened to the wolf?

Some 2,000 years ago there was a large population of wolves in Britain. At that time the land was still heavily forested, and wolves lived in these forests, preying on a wide range of other animals.

Over the next thousand years, early farmers began to clear the forests. As a result, many of the forest-dwelling animals, including the wolf, also started to disappear. By the time the Normans arrived in 1066, many animals had been brought to the point of extinction.

The wolf in particular suffered. Over many centuries stories of the wolf's ferocity had become part of the folklore, and the wolf was now greatly feared. People killed wolves at every opportunity. And the fact that wolves often attacked domestic animals, particularly sheep, meant that they were relentlessly persecuted by farmers.

In the late 1400s an attempt was made to conserve wolves by introducing a closed season — a period of a few months each year, during which wolves could not be hunted. However, it was too late and the wolf disappeared in Britain in about 1550. Wolves survive in Scandinavia and North America, where they are still hunted.

Today wolves survive in North America, Spain and parts of Scandinavia.

In Britain, little remains of the great forests that once covered the land. As a result, several forest animals, such as the wild boar, the brown bear, the beaver and the wolf, have disappeared. Other animals managed to adapt to life in the new habitats that were created as humans changed the landscape — woodlands, meadows, hedgerows, downland and heathland. However, in recent years even these habitats have started to disappear. Downland and moorland are being ploughed up and 'improved' by the use of fertilizers. In the past 40 years over 200,000 kilometres of hedgerow have been removed, because today's mechanized farming is more easily carried out in large fields. Wetlands, which existed at the time of the great forests, are being drained and converted into crop fields.

The story is much the same elsewhere in the world. In every area where humans have established large permanent settlements, they have cleared away the natural vegetation in order to farm the land. In the USA, the great central plains where vast numbers of bison once grazed became today's vast grain growing lands. Today most bison survive in Yellowstone National Park, where they are protected. In the eastern USA, as in Europe, much of the natural broadleaved forest has disappeared.

Plants such as the southern marsh orchid, marsh valerian and marsh marigold have all become rarer in Britain, as the damp meadows they need have been drained for agriculture.

Vast herds of bison formerly roamed the prairies of midwestern America. Today, due to hunting and farming practices, there are no bison on the prairies but a good breeding herd has been established in Yellowstone National Park.

In Australia the same process has taken place over a period of only 200 years, since the arrival of European settlers. Here, it is the native eucalypt forests in the eastern and western parts of the continent that have been cut down. The wheatbelt of Western Australia now occupies an area that formerly supported a rich variety of native eucalypt plants, such as salmon gum, wandoo and York gum. Today, these plants are restricted to a number of small isolated communities. Thirteen of the 46 species of mammal have disappeared from this region and nine of those are now extinct on the Australian mainland.

The western swamp turtle of Australia is now rare because many of the swamps in which it lives have been drained to create agricultural land.

23

Threatened rainforests

Removal of the world's temperate forests has now largely ceased. In some countries lessons have been learned and some attempts are being made to repair the damage and conserve the wildlife that remains. Today, however, it is the world's tropical rainforests that are being threatened. These are the forests that grow in warm, tropical regions where the annual rainfall is high. Rainforests occur in South and Central America, Africa and South-east Asia. There are no seasons in rainforest areas and plants grow almost continuously. As a result, tropical rainforest has become the world's richest environment, supporting a huge variety of life.

Rainforest is being exploited on a large scale. Often huge areas of rainforest are cut down to provide hardwood timbers, such as mahogany or teak. But in many places the forest is cleared by burning to make room for grazing land. In Costa Rica, in Central America, for example, 65,000 hectares of forest are being removed each year in order to provide grazing areas for cattle — cheap beef is a valuable export for this country. At the present rate, all of Costa Rica's rainforest will disappear during the next 20 or 30 years, along with the forests of other countries in Central America. A large proportion of the rainforests of South America, Africa and South-east Asia are also under severe threat.

Unlike temperate forest, rainforest is virtually self-supporting. The nutrients from dead organisms are recycled almost immediately and the soil beneath the forest is therefore very poor. In spite of this, it is possible to farm such land. People living in rainforests carry on a type of farming known as shifting agriculture, similar to the type of agriculture practised in Europe 5,000

Above *The green basilisk of Costa Rica can run across water. This unusual lizard is just one of the thousands of species threatened by the removal of their rainforest habitat.*

Left *In Brazil huge areas of rainforest have been cut down to provide grazing land for beef cattle. Most will eventually be turned into American hamburgers.*

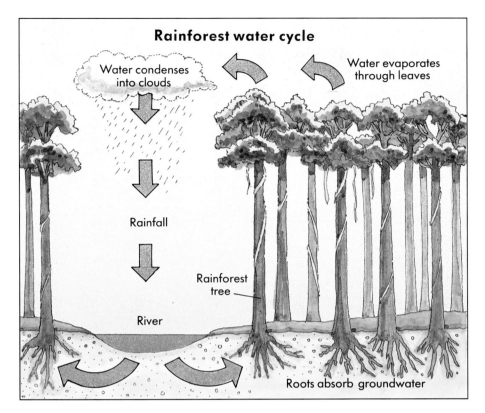

Rainforest water cycle

Water condenses into clouds

Water evaporates through leaves

Rainfall

Rainforest tree

River

Roots absorb groundwater

A rainforest generates its own water cycle. Rain that falls on to the canopy drips down through the undergrowth and into the soil. There the water is rapidly taken up again by the roots of the plants and they release it through their leaves by the process known as transpiration. In the air above the forest, the moisture forms clouds and soon falls as rain again, thus completing the water cycle.

years ago. A small family group clears a small area of forest and farms the exposed land for a few years until the soil is exhausted. Then they move on, and the area they have left begins to regenerate with seed from the surrounding forest. But if the land is cleared on a larger scale, the system breaks down. Without plants to hold it together, the topsoil is washed away by rain.

Tropical forest actually creates its own rainfall. The giant trees have large root systems that soak up the rainwater as soon as it reaches the ground. Later the trees release the moisture from their leaves into the air, where it gathers to form new rain clouds. Without the forest, the rain will cease to fall in these areas, and this will probably result in changes to the climate of other regions. At the same time, it is thought that removal of the rainforest will contribute greatly to the condition known as the greenhouse effect (see page 43).

Thus, the destruction of wildlife habitats, particularly tropical rainforest, has become a serious threat to our planet.

The 10cm long pygmy marmoset of Brazil is the world's smallest monkey. As its forest home has been cleared, it has adapted to life in the maize fields planted by the local people. But if all the rainforest is destroyed, it too will disappear.

Soil and water

Successful farming depends largely on the soil. It should have a good, crumbly texture and contain the nutrients that plants need. There must also be a moderate supply of fresh water. Disturbing the natural balance between a soil, its water supply and plant cover causes problems.

Disappearing soils

Soils need a good covering of plants, because it is the roots of plants that hold the soil particles together. A soil that loses its plant cover becomes exposed to wind and rain and may be rapidly blown or washed away. This condition is known as soil erosion.

Farmers discovered the problem of soil erosion thousands of years ago. They soon learned that on sloping ground rainwater tends to wash exposed soils downhill. On the steepest slopes, the farmers prevented this by cutting flat terraces into the hillsides. Such terraces can still be seen

These rice terraces in the Philippines have survived for 2,000 years. They serve both to hold back the water needed for growing rice and to prevent erosion of the hillsides.

Severely eroded hills in Mexico. When the trees were cut down, the rain washed away the soil.

in several parts of the world. On more gradual slopes, farmers adopted a technique known as contour ploughing, in which the ploughed furrows follow the contours of the ground.

Unfortunately, these practices have not always been carried out. Thirty years ago in Nepal, the steep slopes of the Himalayan foothills were covered with forest. As the population increased, the local people began to clear the forests to provide land for growing food and timber for their cooking fires. Today there is almost no forest left and torrential rains have washed much of the topsoil down to the plains of Bangladesh. There the rivers have become silted up and the land is now much more likely to flood during periods of heavy rain. This was one of the main causes of the devastating flood of 1988. In Nepal, people are now starting to replant the hillsides with trees. However, the problem of flooding in Bangladesh may never be solved.

Soil erosion can happen wherever the soil is left exposed to the elements for too long. For example, the removal of large areas of rainforest has led to severe erosion in nearly all tropical areas. In temperate regions, large, open expanses of heavily-cultivated arable land are very easily eroded by the wind and heavy rains. The farmlands of the USA and Canada lose an amazing 3,000 million tonnes of topsoil each year. Rivers, already polluted by pesticides and chemical fertilizers, become further polluted and silted up with soil. The problem in the USA is now being tackled by the enforcement of new laws. Elsewhere, the problem is getting worse; in India, for example, three quarters of the cultivated land (about half of the country) now suffers serious environmental problems, most of which are due to soil erosion. Even in Britain, soil erosion has become a problem in East Anglia, where most of the land is used for farming. Removal of the hedgerows has left the fields exposed to the winds, which, every year, remove about 18 tonnes of soil from each hectare of land.

In other parts of the world, soil erosion is being caused by a combination of drought and overgrazing. Droughts — long periods during which little or no rain falls — are caused by temporary changes in climate, and the lack of water means that plants cannot grow properly. Crops fail and there is little grazing for domestic animals. Drought is one of the major causes of famine.

Scientists do not fully understand the reasons for such changes. However, overgrazing drought-stricken lands causes severe problems. The animals soon remove what little plant cover there is, with the result that the exposed soil becomes degraded; that is, it starts to blow away and lose its fertility. Much the same thing happens when domestic animals are allowed to overgraze the sparse plant life that grows around the edges of deserts. Overgrazing arid (very dry) land is a problem in North Africa, the Middle East, Australia and parts of Asia. Many people fear that fertile land is turning into desert.

Sudanese nomads move from place to place with their animals. The drier areas with less vegetation quickly become overgrazed.

The American Dust Bowl

During the 1930s the central part of the American corn belt became so badly eroded that crops could no longer be grown. Drought combined with excessive cultivation caused the soil to turn to dust, which was then blown away in huge quantities by the wind. Crops would not grow and cattle died of starvation. Chickens and other poultry birds died in the dust storms, while people suffered from dust fever. Farmers in Colorado, Kansas, Oklahoma and New Mexico were forced to leave their homes and their land and move elsewhere.

The creation of the American Dust Bowl is regarded as one of the worst environmental blunders in recorded history. Fifty years later, this land has recovered sufficently to grow crops again. However, soil erosion continues to be a serious problem and today an even greater area appears to be under threat. The lesson of the 1930s does not seem to have been learned.

*Drought and overcultivation caused the Dust Bowl of the 1930s. Many farmers abandoned their homes as their fields turned to dust (**below**). The severe drought of 1988 (**above**) left many American farmers fearing the same could happen again.*

Watering the land

Fresh water is essential for plant growth and, in places where rainfall is low, it has to be supplied by irrigating the land. About 12% of the world's farmland is irrigated, and this land produces up to 30% of the world's harvest. Irrigation is a very old technique; it was practised by the early farmers of Mesopotamia (now Iraq). Carried out sensibly, it causes no difficulties, but excessive irrigation can result in serious problems.

Because irrigation is used in places where rain falls infrequently, it has to be done with water that has been stored. In many places it is done using groundwater — rainwater that has seeped down into the ground to form an underground reserve. In some places, however, the groundwater is being used up faster than it is being replaced. A large area of land in Texas and neighbouring

A huge mechanical sprinkler trundles slowly through a field in Utah, USA, to irrigate the crops.

states of the USA has been turned into productive farmland by using water from a huge underground store. But this is being used up at an ever-increasing rate. When the reserves run out, the land above will become dry and barren.

Another problem that is becoming increasingly common is that irrigated soils are becoming saltier, or more saline; the problem is called salinization. This is not a new process — it happened in Mesopotamia thousands of years ago and may have been one of the reasons why the early Sumerian civilization collapsed.

All soils contain some salts, and groundwaters therefore contain salts washed out of soils. In hot climates water evaporates quickly, leaving the remaining water with a higher salt content.

Groundwater used for irrigation evaporates from the ground, leaving the salts behind in the topsoil. Over a period of time, the soil becomes more and more salty, and in some cases this can lead to the ground becoming hard and useless. In Australia there are 3,000 square kilometres of barren, salt-laden ground.

Salt may also be carried up from below. Subsoils often contain high levels of salts washed down from above over millions of years. Excessive irrigation of badly drained soils raises the water table (the level of the water in the ground), bringing these salts to the surface. Very badly drained soils may become waterlogged. Salinization and waterlogging of irrigated land are now serious problems in many countries, including Pakistan, Egypt, Iraq, India and USA.

Right *Salinization is an increasing problem in Egypt. Over-irrigation leads to waterlogging of the soil which brings salts to the surface.*

Below *The traditional method of irrigating crops is by means of water-filled channels, such as this one in Egypt.*

Producing the world's food

Many of the methods now being used to produce the world's food cause direct harm to the environment. At the same time, they can also cause problems indirectly. Even some of today's problems concerned with human health can be traced back to farming practices.

The Green Revolution

As the population of the world has increased, it has been the policy of governments all over the world to produce large amounts of food as cheaply as possible. Unfortunately, it is this very policy that has caused many of the problems facing the environment.

During the 1960s and 1970s, many of the world's developing countries took part in what was called the 'Green Revolution'. The aim was to grow large quantities of important food crops, such as wheat and maize, using new strains of each crop, specially developed for the purpose. Food production did increase, but there were problems. Large amounts of fertilizer were needed to make the crops grow, but artificial fertilizers are expensive and, in many cases, farmers in developing countries could not afford them. Vast quantities of pesticides were needed to control insect pests, with the result that water courses became polluted. Growing the same crops over vast areas of land also allowed crop diseases to spread more easily. In addition, the new crops needed more water than traditional ones, and the increasing demand for irrigation led to salinization in many areas. Human diseases carried by small animals that live in water also spread rapidly.

Cocoa is a cash crop grown in many developing countries. As with other cash crops, insecticides are used to control insect pests.

The problems were made worse by the fact that many governments exported the food that was grown, in order to bring in foreign money. Local farmers remained poor and hungry. In some parts of the world farmers grew cash crops, such as peanuts, instead . of more important foods. Without a great deal of fertilizer, peanuts soon exhaust the land and so farmers began to cultivate land normally used for grazing animals. In North Africa nomadic tribes were forced to graze their animals on the driest land at the edge of the desert, and this inevitably led to overgrazing.

Another problem associated with the Green Revolution, and also with modern farming in

Pineapples grown in Kenya. Such cash crops earn money for developing countries, but take up land that could grow crops for local people.

general, is that farmers and growers tend to favour just a few popular crop varieties. The problem is that if the less popular varieties are allowed to disappear completely, their genetic make-up will become unavailable to us. This is not just unfortunate; it is potentially disastrous. A diverse and varied store of genetic resources is essential. For example, if an important crop variety fails because of a new disease, it is possible to breed a new disease-resistant variety by using genes from a similar crop species.

Right Battery chickens in Georgia, USA. Eggs produced in this way are relatively cheap, but many people think that it is unacceptable to confine birds in small cages.

Left In the temperate countries of the northern hemisphere large amounts of food can be grown. In the wheat plains of Saskatchewan, Canada, the grain is stored in huge 'elevators'.

Below In Ethiopia farmers grow and sell relatively small amounts of food. However, many more crop varieties are grown here. Ethiopia is, in fact, a source area for many of the world's food crops.

Food mountains and famines

The same policies of cheap food production have been carried out elsewhere in the world. In temperate climates crop-growing is easier, and farmers in the developed countries can usually afford to use fertilizers. As a result, many of the world's developed countries now have a surplus of food. The USA exports vast amounts of grain to other countries, including the USSR. In Europe, the European Economic Community (EEC) adopted a policy of maintaining food prices, even when excess food is produced. The purpose of this policy is to make sure that Europe never runs out of food. However, because farmers have been encouraged to overproduce, huge amounts of surplus grain, meat and dairy products have accumulated. Reducing these food 'mountains' has become a major problem.

   In other parts of the world, people are starving as a result of famines. Food can be and has been

transported to famine areas. But transporting too much food to such places can make the problem worse in the long term. Governments of developing countries usually have to pay for the food, and sometimes this may damage the country's economy.

Food and health

In recent years we have become increasingly conscious of the connection between the food we eat and our health. Foods that contain large amounts of animal fats are now regarded as less desirable. Milk and cheese, which were formerly praised for their food value, are now much less popular, and today's consumers now demand leaner meat. Animals are therefore fed on high protein feeds that include such ingredients as soya and meat products.

At the same time, farming has become more and more intensive. Some farm animals, notably chickens and pigs, are now reared indoors in huge numbers. They are given concentrated feeds designed to make them grow as rapidly as possible. Such farming methods are aimed at quantity, rather than quality, with the result that today's food is much less nutritious than it could be. Chicken, for example, was originally promoted as being a lean meat. But today's chickens, reared indoors on concentrated foods in just six weeks, contain a high proportion of fat.

Intensive farming has also been criticized for other reasons. Chickens are kept in battery cages or in densely-packed sheds. Pigs and calves are often reared in small pens, in which they have little room to move around. Many people believe that it is unacceptably cruel to rear animals in this way. Another problem is that disease spreads more easily when animals are crowded together. To counter this, animals have to be given large amounts of antibiotic. In the USA, antibiotics are added to feed, and this assists growth. The problem is that diseases then become resistant to the antibiotics and are very difficult to treat.

Drug-resistant organisms could pose a serious risk to human health. In 1984, scientists in the USA found that meat contaminated with the organism salmonella had caused 18 people to suffer food poisoning; one victim died. In Britain it has been known for many years that chickens contain salmonella. When chicken is properly cooked, the salmonella organisms are killed, and the problem was not thought to be too serious. Recently, however, salmonella in hens used for egg production has become the cause of some concern, as there appears to be a very small risk of the organism finding its way into eggs. The British government advised some people, such as small children, pregnant women and elderly people, not to eat any foods containing raw eggs.

Today a wide variety of pre-packed meats are available to suit increasingly health-conscious consumers.

Good health and nutrition are very important. Many people now give more thought to the kinds of food that they and their children eat.

An intensive beef-raising unit in Arkansas, USA. The animals are fed entirely on concentrate feed, to which antibiotics have been added. The use of antibiotics is not permitted in Europe.

Another disease that is currently causing concern is known as bovine spongiform encephalopathy (BSE), a brain disease of cattle. This is a fatal disease, for which there is no known cure. It develops slowly, but affected cattle show no symptoms until the disease is in its later stages. It is similar to a sheep disease called scrapie and also to two human brain diseases, although there is as yet no evidence that these diseases are linked, or that BSE can be passed on to humans.

The point is, however, that both salmonella and BSE may be spread by the practice of using meat products in animal feeds. Scientists are now trying to establish whether or not BSE poses any risk to human health.

As a result of all these problems, some people are now questioning the wisdom of a cheap food policy. Instead, they believe that food production should be based above all on human health considerations, as it is in Sweden.

Farming for the future

Farming is a vital occupation. Everyone in the world needs food, and the only alternative to farming would be for us all to return to the hunting and gathering way of life practised by our ancestors 10,000 years ago. Clearly, this would be impossible, and farmers must, therefore, be allowed to farm, and make a reasonable profit from their land.

However, as we have seen, farming can and does have an adverse effect upon the environment; habitat destruction, pollution, desertification and salinization have all been associated with farming for thousands of years. Today, the situation is getting worse, and there is clearly an urgent need to tackle the problems now. Landowners and farmers should realize that their ownership is only temporary; what they do now will affect the land for perhaps thousands of years to come. We and they owe it to future generations to ensure that the planet remains a pleasant place in which to live.

Agriculture and the human population

'. . . . it is already appararent that the rate of increase in the production of food in some parts of Africa has been overtaken by the rate of consumption due to the increase in the human population.

'The unpalatable fact is that agriculture has been the victim of its own success. The effects of its own activities, and the effects of the activities of the huge human population it has succeeded in supporting, have caused the biggest of all external disturbances to the ecology of this globe.'

H.R.H. The Duke of Edinburgh in 'The Richard Dimbleby Lecture', broadcast on BBC1 on 7 March 1989.

Seeds in a seed bank remain viable for only a limited period. Supplies of new seeds are continually needed. Here scientists are testing the viability of wheat seeds in a Mexican seed bank.

A better approach to farming

The picture is not entirely black, as positive action is being taken. In some countries, seed banks have been set up, in an attempt to save the genetic material contained in crop plants that are no longer popular. Many pests can now be controlled using biological means rather than pesticides. In the most common form of biological control, the numbers of a pest species are kept down to a reasonable level by introducing a natural predator or disease-causing organism. For example, sugar cane scale insects can be controlled by a species of ladybird — the ladybirds simply eat them! Black vine weevils are controlled by introducing parasitic worms, and scientists are experimenting with a virus to control codling moth (whose caterpillars are a pest of apple trees). Biological control does not always work and in some cases the controlling organism may itself become a pest. However, many pesticides are now found to be ineffective and, in general, biological control has a much greater chance of success than a new pesticide.

Left Most ladybirds feed on both the larvae and adults of aphids. Introducing ladybirds is therefore an excellent way of controlling these crop pests.

Right Not all attempts at biological control are successful. The marine toad, or cane toad, was introduced into Australia in the early 1900s to control the sugar cane beetle on which it normally feeds in its native home of South America. Unfortunately, this poisonous toad failed to control the beetle, but it bred rapidly and is now a nuisance in the cane-growing areas of Australia.

Poppies and chamomile thriving in a strip around the edge of a German rye field that was not sprayed with herbicides.

Farmers, too, are now becoming actively involved in conservation. In Britain, for example, some farmers are replanting hedges. Some arable farmers now leave strips of unploughed grassland around their fields; these act as havens for wildlife. Broadleaved woodlands are being grown as a long-term crop. In northern India the Chipko movement, started in the early 1970s, has saved the forests from being destroyed. And in Kenya the Green Belt movement is concerned with managing the whole environment, from the soil to the climate. In other developing countries some farmers are returning to traditional methods of agriculture, using crops suited to local conditions that do not require expensive fertilizers or pesticides.

The 'organic' alternative

Many farmers still regard the use of chemical fertilizers and pesticides as essential. However, much more is now known about how plants take up fertilizers, and now they can be applied in a way that ensures that very little is washed away. On the other hand, in Britain and Europe, a number of farmers have abandoned the use of artificial fertilizers and pesticides altogether. Instead they have gone over to the system known as organic farming. Food produced by organic farming methods is more expensive, but many people are convinced that it is necessary and that it will become economic in the future. Organic farming uses natural materials, such as manures

What is 'organic'?

The term 'organic' has come to have several slightly different meanings, which is sometimes a little confusing. Strictly speaking, the word 'organic' should refer to a material that forms part of, or is derived from, a living organism. Thus any dead plant or animal material is organic. Materials that are not related to living organisms, such as rocks and minerals, are called inorganic.

Organic chemicals include most pesticides, such as the organochlorines.

Today the term 'organic' is used by environmentalists to describe something that is natural, as opposed to something that is synthetic (made by humans). This definition clearly excludes all artificial pesticides and fertilizers. Organic farmers use organic materials such as composts and manures. But some inorganic materials are also acceptable in organic farming. For example, some organic fertilizers contain Chilean nitrate, a naturally-occurring rock fertilizer.

and composts, which keep the soil supplied with nutrients and improve the structure of the soil. Soil fertility is helped by a system of planting called crop rotation, in which an area is planted with a different crop each year. Crop rotation also helps to keep down the numbers of pest animals. In organic farming, only pesticides based on natural substances are used.

Concern for the environment

Over the past thirty years the importance of the environment has become more and more apparent. Organizations like Friends of the Earth, the Worldwide Fund for Nature (formerly the World Wildlife Fund) and the Soil Association have raised a wide range of environmental issues, among which are many directly connected with farming. In Britain, other organizations, such as the National Trust, The Council for the Protection of Rural England and a number of local conservation trusts devote large sums of money towards saving the most important natural sites

Right A Farming and Wildlife advisor discusses with a farmer the importance of preserving trees on his farmland.

before they are destroyed. Similar organizations are found in countries all over the world.

However, really major changes can only be achieved by governments. Much needs to be done, but politicians in many parts of the world are now realizing the need for action.

In Britain, Farming and Wildlife Advisory Groups (FWAGs) have been set up in most counties; advisors are invited by farmers to visit their farms to suggest how wildlife conservation can be carried out alongside farming enterprises.

Governments in Europe are now looking for ways of reducing food surpluses by encouraging or even forcing farmers to produce less. One idea being proposed in Britain is that every year a certain proportion of today's arable land should be left unsown — a scheme known as set-aside. However, such a scheme seems unlikely to be of much benefit to wildlife or the environment and may not even work.

Another strategy adopted by some governments is to encourage farmers to find alternative uses for some of their land. The unwanted farmland could be used as recreation areas for people or for some necessary housing. Conservation groups are hoping that some former fields will be left to regenerate into natural grassland or scrub, or that they will be planted with a variety of broadleaved trees. In time, such areas would become much-needed habitats for plants and animals.

Future prospects

At present the major problems concerning agriculture and the environment remain unsolved; and they are not likely to be solved in the near future. The world's human population is growing, and there is evidence to suggest that there may come a stage when the demand for food exceeds what can be grown. In countries like Ethiopia this is already happening, with catastrophic results: famine, disease and great human suffering.

Thus the pressure on the environment seems likely to increase rather than decrease. At the same time, the need to produce more food will very probably create additional problems. Genetic engineering, for example, is already an issue that is causing some argument. Scientists can now alter the genetic make-up of an organism. This means that it may soon be possible to create cereal crop plants that, like pea and bean plants, can make use of the nitrogen that is in the air. It may also become easier to create disease-resistant varieties of crops. Environmentalists are opposed to such techniques; they believe that the dangers of releasing harmful organisms into the environment are too great.

Spraying strawberries with a solution containing an experimental, genetically-altered bacterium intended to help the plants resist frost damage. The results of this American experiment were promising.

Some problems can be solved by individual countries. However, problems that are causing changes in the world's atmosphere and climate affect us all and will probably be solved only by international agreement. An obvious example is the destruction of the world's rainforests. Experts believe that, if the process of burning and clearing these forests is allowed to continue for much longer, it will almost certainly contribute a great deal to the greenhouse effect.

The greenhouse effect

Heat from the sun sustains life on earth. It travels through space in the form of infrared, or heat, rays. This enters the earth's atmosphere, warming the air, the sea and the land.

Heat rays from the sun pass through glass. In a greenhouse they are absorbed by the plants, which then give out heat themselves. But the heat rays given out by the plants have longer wavelengths and cannot pass through glass. They are therefore reflected back into the greenhouse, which then warms up.

A similar process happens in the atmosphere. As the sun's heat rays warm up the plants, soil and water on the surface of the earth, they too give out heat rays that have longer wavelengths. The atmosphere is not, of course, surrounded by glass! But certain gases in the atmosphere have the same effect and prevent the longer wavelength heat from escaping. The most important 'greenhouse' gas is carbon dioxide, although others, such as methane,

also play a part.

Carbon dioxide is 'breathed out' by all living organisms and is produced when any fuel or organic material burns. It is also taken in and used by green plants in the food-making process known as photosynthesis. Thus, under normal conditions, the amount of carbon dioxide in the atmosphere is kept at a steady level. In recent years, however, the burning of fossil fuels (coal, oil and the fuels derived from them) has caused an increase in the level of carbon dioxide in the atmosphere. At the same time, the temperature of the Earth's atmosphere does appear to be rising and many people are now convinced that a serious problem is occurring.

It has been calculated that the temperature of the atmosphere could increase by over 4°C by the year 2050. In comparison, the temperature of the Earth's atmosphere has only risen by 4°C over the last 10,000 years. The results of such a rapid warming are difficult to predict, but it seems certain that the Earth's environment will be drastically altered.

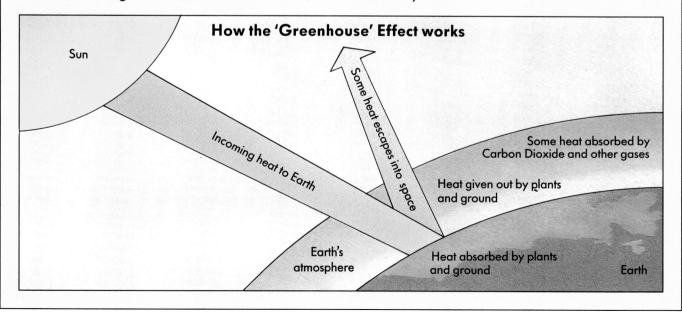

How the 'Greenhouse' Effect works

Sun

Incoming heat to Earth

Some heat escapes into space

Earth's atmosphere

Some heat absorbed by Carbon Dioxide and other gases

Heat given out by plants and ground

Heat absorbed by plants and ground

Earth

Left In Panama, as in most tropical regions of the world, rainforest is being destroyed at an alarming rate.

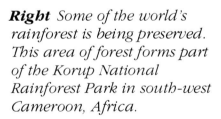

Right Some of the world's rainforest is being preserved. This area of forest forms part of the Korup National Rainforest Park in south-west Cameroon, Africa.

To the people of the countries in which rainforests grow, they are a valuable asset that can provide a much-needed source of income. Thus in order to save these forests, it would appear to be essential that alternative sources of income are found. In Britain farmers are now compensated for leaving SSSIs (Sites of Special Scientific Interest) alone. Perhaps this idea should be applied on an international scale. The only way to save the world's remaining rainforests may be for the developed countries to pay the owners of these forests not to destroy them, and to help such countries develop alternative sources of income.

If the rainforests are not saved and the atmosphere warms up due to the greenhouse effect, the whole world may suffer. A warmer climate will mean that agriculture will change all over the world; deserts will form in many of the areas where food is grown today. Sea levels may rise if the polar ice caps melt, thus further reducing the land area on which food can be grown. In these circumstances we may, perhaps, continue to feed the world's population, but we will probably destroy the natural environment in the process. If the environment does not survive, neither will we. Action is needed now, before it is too late.

Glossary

Antibiotic A natural drug produced by a mould (a fungus) that is used to treat bacterial infections.

Bacteria (singular: bacterium) A large group of tiny, one-celled organisms. Some cause disease; others break down dead plant or animal material.

Biocide A chemical used to kill a living organism, such as a fungus, a weed plant or an insect pest.

Broadleaved Trees that have broad leaves (as opposed to needles), that are shed each autumn.

Cash crops Certain crops grown by one country to sell to another.

Climate The conditions of temperature, wind and rainfall that generally apply in a particular area.

Compost Plant material, sometimes mixed with manure, that has been allowed to rot down into a crumbly mixture.

Decompose To break down a substance, helping it to rot away.

Desert A region of low rainfall, usually characterized by water-conserving plants and specially adapted animals.

Desertification A process in which dry grassland or scrubland becomes more like desert. The process is usually associated with drought conditions and may be accelerated by overgrazing by domestic or wild animals.

Domesticated Kept as livestock for humans.

Drought A period when little or no rain falls.

Effluent A waste liquid formed during an industrial, farming or waste treatment process.

Environment All the conditions that surround us, including the atmosphere, climate, other animals and plants and the type of soil and rock.

Erosion The wearing away or removal of rock or soil by the action of wind or water.

Eutrophication The process by which still water supplied with large amounts of nutrient chemicals becomes starved of oxygen.

Famine A situation in which the food supply is much too low to feed the existing population, with the result that many people starve to death.

Fertility (of soil or land) The ability to sustain a large number of growing plants.

Fertilizer A substance, such as a manure or a chemical, used to enrich a soil.

Genetic Concerned with genes, the factors in an animal or plant that control all its characteristics. Genes are passed on from parent to offspring.

Green Revolution The attempt during the 1960s and 1970s to increase the amount of food grown in developing countries by the use of high-yielding crop varieties.

Groundwater Rainwater that has penetrated the surface of the ground and become stored in soil or underground rocks.

Habitat The living area of an animal or plant. Meadows, hedgerows and ponds are all habitats.

Hybrid A plant that has resulted from the breeding of two genetically different parents. Usually hybrids cannot reproduce.

Insecticide A substance designed to kill one or more types of insect.

Irrigation The introduction of water into dry soils by means of surface channels or by the use of pipes and sprinklers.

Manure A mixture of animal dung and a plant material, such as straw.

Nitrate A chemical whose molecules contain a nitrogen atom linked to three oxygen atoms ($-NO_3$).

Nitrite A chemical whose molecules contain a nitrogen atom linked to two oxygen atoms ($-NO_2$).

Nomadic (of groups of people) Moving from place to place in order to find food and water, and grazing land for animals.

Nutrient A chemical substance that a plant or animal can use in order to grow.

Overgrazing Allowing too many animals to graze land, with the result that the plants are removed or cannot regrow.

Pesticide A substance used to kill one or more animal pests. The term 'pesticide' is also sometimes incorrectly used instead of 'biocide'.

Pollutant A substance that, when released into the environment, causes harm.

Pollution The release into the environment of a substance that causes harm to plants and animals.

Rainforest Forest that grows in the warm, tropical parts of the world where the rainfall is high.

Regeneration (of a forest) The process by which forest plants recolonize land that has been cleared.

Salinization The process by which a soil becomes too salty to support plant life.

Salmonella A type of bacterium that usually causes food poisoning.

Scrapie A disease of sheep that affects the nervous system.

Sewage Semi-liquid waste matter from homes and factories. Treated sewage and material from cesspits is often spread on land as a fertilizer.

Silage Plant material that has been fermented by bacteria in the absence of air. The sugars in the plant material are converted to an acid, which acts as a preservative. Silage is made from grass, clover, kale, pea plants and maize.

Slurry A semi-liquid waste material composed mainly of animal dung and urine.

Subsoil The layer of soil and other material underneath the topsoil.

Topsoil The uppermost, fertile layer of soil from which plants obtain most or all of their nutrients.

Virus A disease-causing organism.

Further reading

Banks, M., *Conserving Rainforests* (Wayland, 1989).

Crawford P., *The Living Isles* (BBC Publications, 1986).

Durrell L., *State of the Ark* (The Bodley Head, 1986).

H.R.H. The Duke of Edinburgh, *Living off the Land* (BBC Publications, 1989).

Goldsmith E. and Hildyard N. (General Editors) *The Earth Report* (Mitchell Beazley, 1988).

Lambert M., *Let's Discuss Pollution* (Wayland, 1988).

Mabey, R., *The Common Ground* (Hutchinson, 1980).

Myers N. (General Editor), *The Gaia Atlas of Planet Management* (Good Books, 1985).

Rickard, G., *20th Century Farming* (Wayland, 1988).

Singer A., *Battle for the Planet* (Pan Books, 1987).

Whitlock R., *The Shaping of the Countryside* (Robert Hale, 1979).

Picture acknowledgements

The publishers would like to thank the following for allowing their photographs to be reproduced in this book: Bruce Coleman Ltd *cover* (Fritz Prenzel), 4 (Nicholas Devore), 7 below (Roger Wilmshurst), 9 left (Dennis Green), 9 right (N. Blake), 11 (Frieder Sauer), 18 (Hans Reinhard); Flour Advisory Bureau 5; FWAG/Helen Simonson 41; Hulton-Deutsch Collection 29 below; Hutchison Library 16 (Sarah Errington), 24 below, 27 (Taylor), 31 above, 38 (Dr. Nigel Smith), 44 below (P. Parker); Mark Lambert 13, 14, 19 below; Oxford Scientific Films 7 above and 8 (Terry Heathcote), 9 above (Colin Milkins), 19 above (Ronald Toms), 23 below (Babs and Bert Wells), 24 above (Michael Fogden), 25 (Michael Dick), 35 (Zigmund Leszczynski), 39 above (Raymond Blythe), 39 below (Kathie Atkinson), 44 above (J. Devries); Topham Picture Library 12, 29 above, 30 (John Griffin), 32, 33, 34 above and below, 42 below; ZEFA 6, 10, 15 (Tortoli), 20 (Heintges), 21, 22, 23 above, 26, 28 (Zingel), 31 below (F. Damm), 36, 37 (Kummels), 40 (Streichan). The illustrations are by Stephen Wheele.

Useful addresses

Australian Association for Environmental Education
GPO Box 112
Canberra ACT 2601
Australia

Council for Environmental Education
School of Education
University of Reading
Reading RG1 5AQ
England

Environment and Conservation Organizations of New Zealand (ECO)
P.O. Box 11057
Wellington
New Zealand

Farming and Wildlife Trust
National Agriculture Centre
Stoneleigh
Near Kenilworth
Warwickshire CV8 2RX
England

Fauna and Flora Preservation Society
79-83 North Street
Brighton BN1 1ZA
England

Friends of the Earth
26-28 Underwood Street
London N1 7JQ
England

Friends of the Earth (Australia)
National Liaison Office
366 Smith Street
Collingwood
Victoria 3065

Friends of the Earth (Canada)
Suite 53
54 Queen Street
Ottawa KP5CS

Friends of the Earth (NZ)
Nagal House
Courthouse Lane
PO Box 39/065
Auckland West

Greenpeace (UK)
30-31 Islington Street
London N1 8XE

Greenpeace (USA)
1611 Connecticut Avenue N.W.
Washington DC2009

Greenpeace (Australia)
310 Angas Street
Adelaide 5000

Greenpeace (Canada)
2623 West 4th Avenue
Vancouver BCV6K 1P8

Watch
22 The Green
Nettleham
Lincs LN2 2NR
England

World Wide Fund for Nature
WWF Information and Education Division
1196 Gland
Switzerland

Index